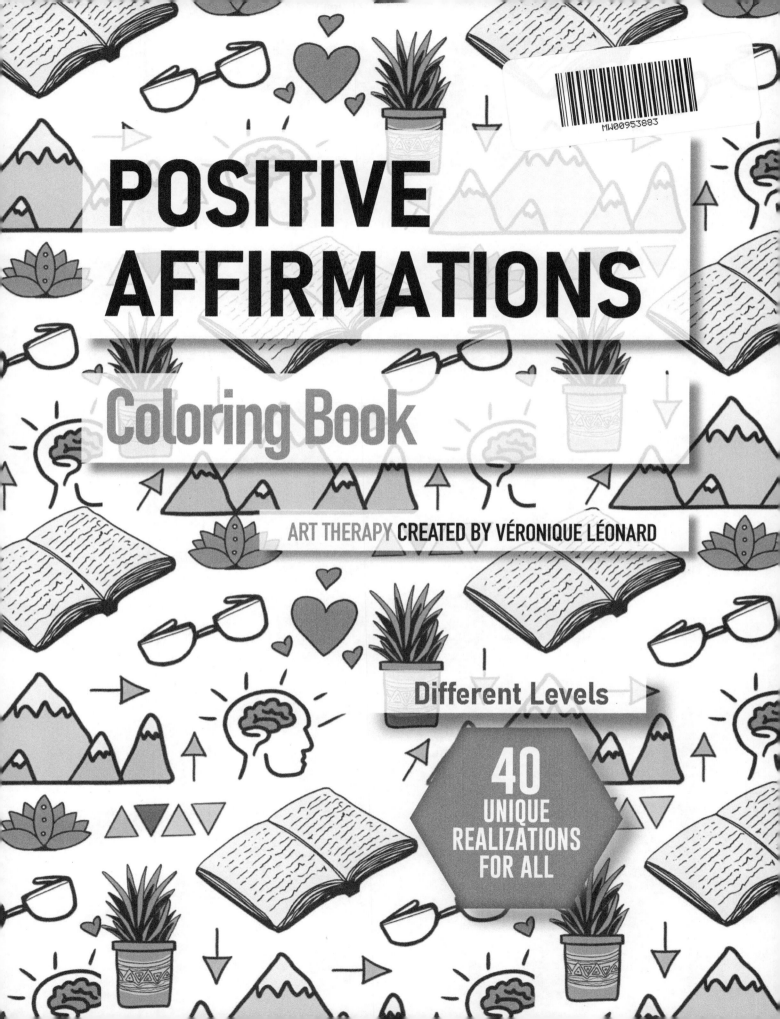

POSITIVE AFFIRMATIONS

Coloring Book

ART THERAPY CREATED BY VÉRONIQUE LÉONARD

Different Levels

40 UNIQUE REALIZATIONS FOR ALL

This book belongs to :

_____

OTHER BOOKS
BY THE SAME AUTHOR

Unique drawings created by the author
in each coloring book!

AFFIRMATIONS POSITIVES

Coloring book for everyone!

FREE YOUR MIND & DEVEOP YOUR CREATIVITY

Coloring is one of the tools of art therapy that offers an individual the opportunity to externalize their emotions and thoughts. This process allows one to clear one's head and move towards positive personal development.

In addition, it is a way to meditate and calm the mind. When you practice drawing regularly, you learn to master the art of coloring. Give yourself the time and space to relax.

ESCAPE TO A WONDERFUL WORD OF COLORS

BEAUTIFUL DRAWINGS OF DIFFERENT LEVELS

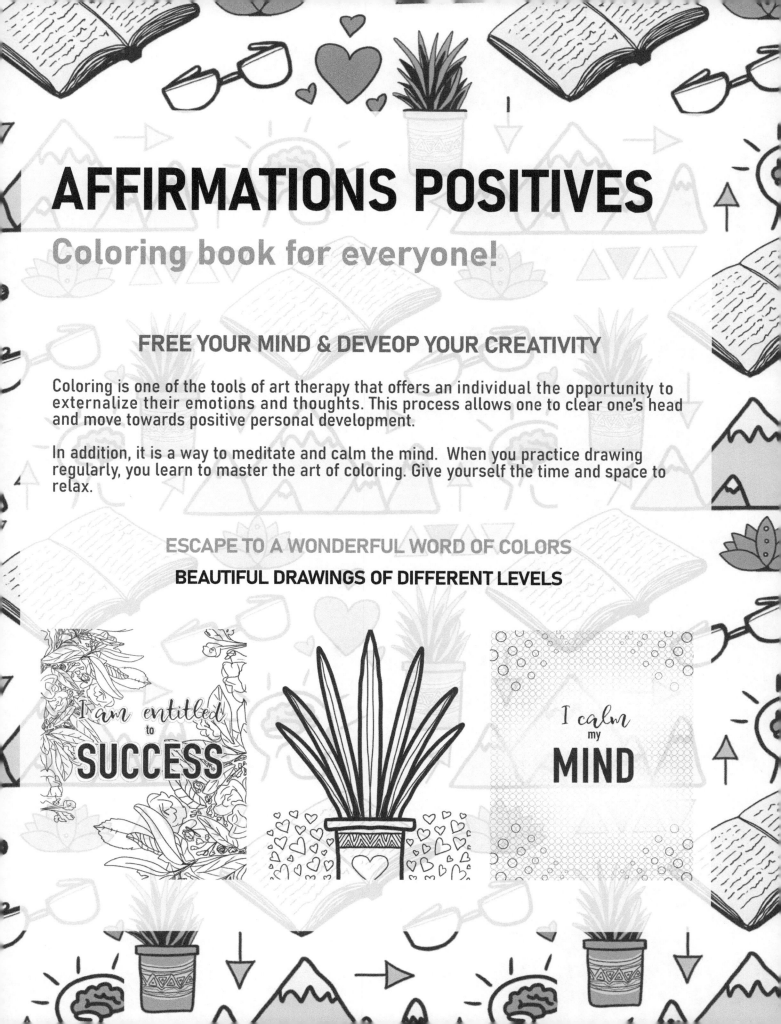

I am entitled to SUCCESS

I calm my MIND

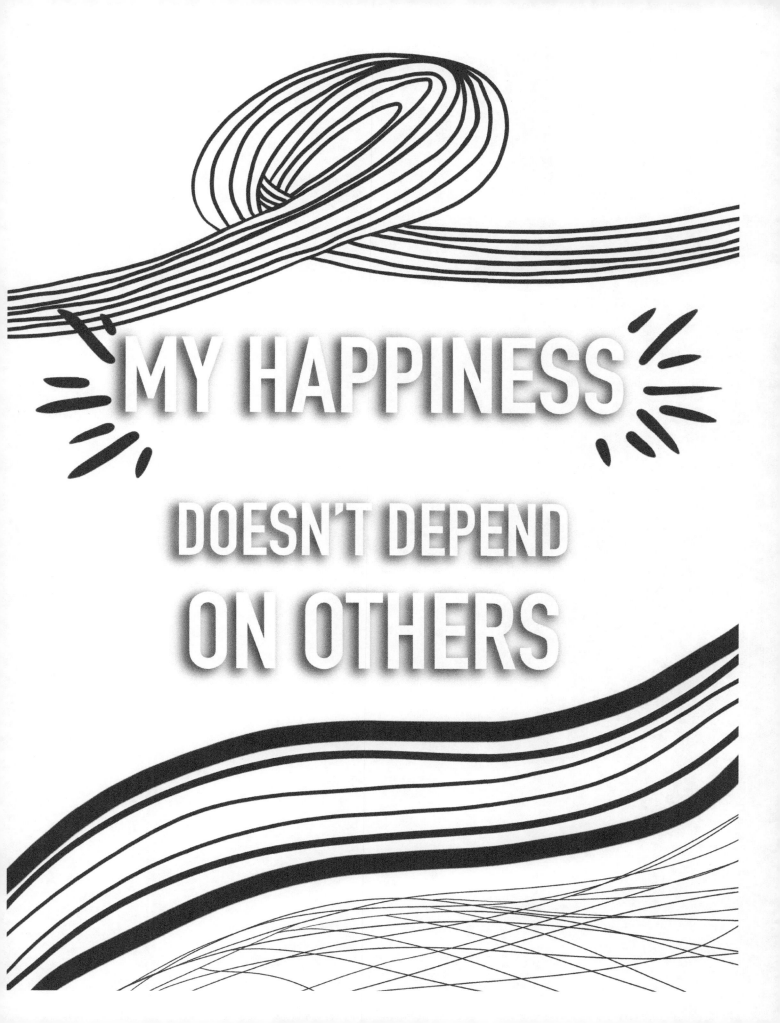

I welcome my emotions

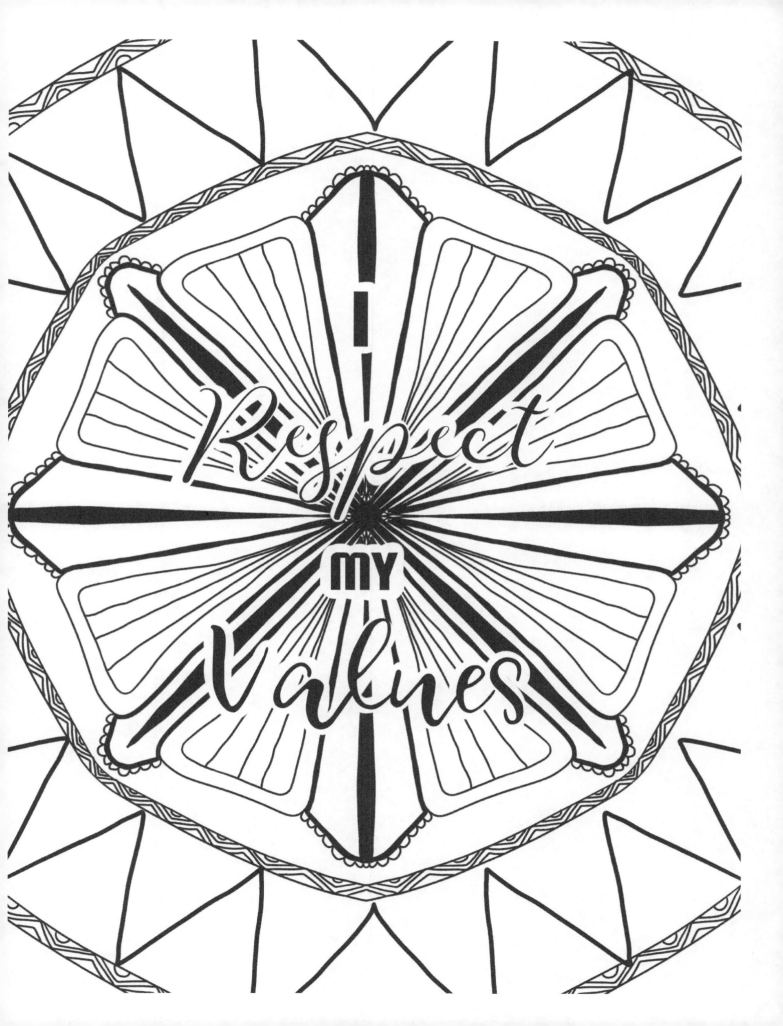

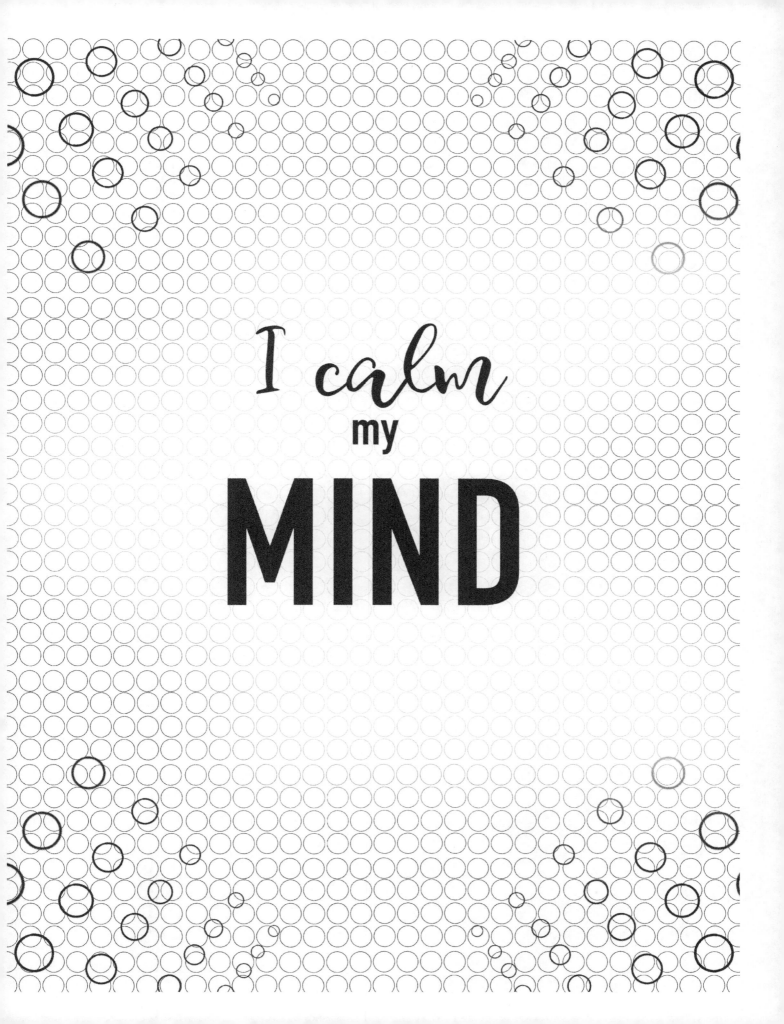

BEING WELL

Surrounded

IS PRICELESS

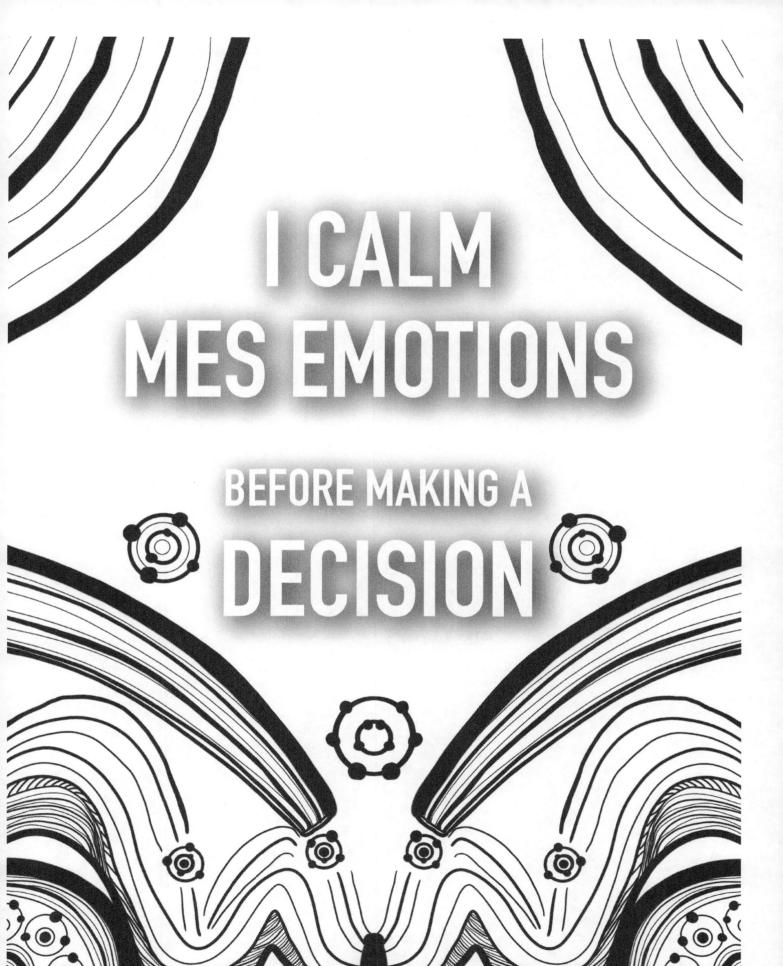

I BREATH
IN & OUT

I try

SOMETHING

NEW

Made in the USA
Las Vegas, NV
23 December 2024